INTRODUCTION TO
AVIATION

Fred Mabonga

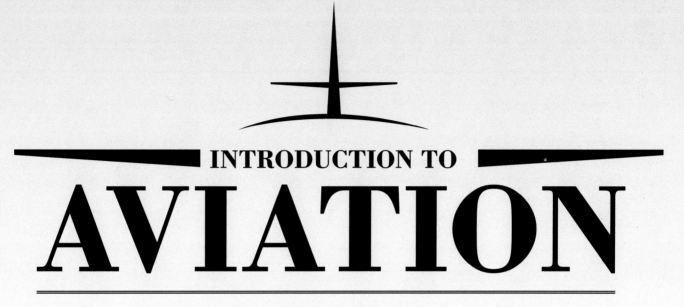

INTRODUCTION TO AVIATION

Fred Mabonga

AuthorHouse™
1663 Liberty Drive
Bloomington, IN 47403
www.authorhouse.com
Phone: 1 (800) 839-8640

Published by AuthorHouse 02/19/2015

ISBN: 978-1-4969-6995-8 (sc)
ISBN: 978-1-4969-7012-1 (e)

Library of Congress Control Number: 2015902587

Print information available on the last page.

Any people depicted in stock imagery provided by Thinkstock are models,
and such images are being used for illustrative purposes only.
Certain stock imagery © Thinkstock.

Because of the dynamic nature of the Internet, any web addresses or links contained in this book may have changed
since publication and may no longer be valid. The views expressed in this work are solely those of the author and do not
necessarily reflect the views of the publisher, and the publisher hereby disclaims any responsibility for them.

This book is dedicated to my two daughters, Kakai Lakeri Mabonga and Judith Nabifo Mabonga, my princesses, who inspired me through their outstanding abilities and brilliance.

Acknowledgements

I would like to acknowledge the very many people I have had the pleasure of dealing with throughout my carrier in aviation. Starting from my days as an aviation student to my many years of working experience in various aviation organisations in different countries, I have interacted with numerous professionals who have made meaningful contributions to my professional abilities.

I look back with admiration to all my lecturers and instructors who imparted knowledge and skills and who had the confidence in me to become an aviation professional.

Looking back at my training days in the United Kingdom and the several industry-type courses from various aircraft manufacturers of different aircraft types, I can only be thankful for the knowledge I have gained over the years.

During my days as a technical instructor developing training programs for various airlines and organisations, I played my part in imparting the knowledge and skills to the next generation of aviation professionals.

In writing this book, I wanted to reach as many people as possible who needed to know something about aviation as well as those contemplating a career in aviation.

I am grateful for all the men and women in aviation with whom I have come in contact and shared many experiences in making aviation safe and a worthwhile vocation.

In furthering aviation safety, I would like to acknowledge Gordon Dupont, the founder of System Safety Services in Canada, with whom I have worked to make to make aviation safe. Known as the Father of the Dirty Dozen, Human Factors Training style, Gordon's work has taken him around the world teaching aviation safety so people can avoid mistakes they never intend to make. It is Gordon's and my wish that we shall make a breakthrough in achieving total aviation safety, especially in regions of the world such as Africa, where achieving aviation safety has been a huge challenge. In acknowledging Gordon's work, I hope that other men and women in aviation will join us in making a contribution to achieving and upholding aviation safety.

Heartfelt thanks to the following special people:

Joyce Nkuwa Mabonga (airline professional, retired crew): You stood by me in a special way during the writing of this book and while burning of the midnight oil. Thanks for your words of encouragement and great nutrition!

Sister Rose Nambozo: You are amazing! You made all this possible and constantly pushed me to publish in the United States. You are a great sponsor with strong words of encouragement.

Nkweto (Liz) Mfula (airline professional, retired crew): You made a big contribution to keep the lights on during writing. Thank you for your words of encouragement.

Mary Luembe (airline professional, retired crew): Thank you for your constant words of encouragement.

Foreword

Aviation is a strictly regulated industry. It has to be this way because of the risks involved in all activities within various sectors of the industry. The safe and efficient transportation of people and goods by air is no easy task.

The high cost of investment in the aviation industry operations dictates that care must be taken to ensure minimum loss. This investment includes the high cost of training the aviation professionals to carry out their critical tasks. The training of pilots, aircraft engineers, air traffic controllers, and others is a huge investment. The cost of equipment, such as aircraft, maintenance hangars and workshops, tooling for aircraft maintenance, air traffic control towers, and operational equipment (including the tooling to maintain the operational equipment), is also high. Therefore, regulations, rules, and procedures must be strictly followed to prevent damage, loss, or harm.

Operators of aircraft and airports ensure that all regulations are followed to achieve the mission of operation. This adherence to regulations ensures that no operating crew is hurt, no aircraft is damaged or destroyed, no avoidable incidents and/or accidents occur, and that the aim to achieve a safe and efficient air transportation system is realised.

All aviation sectors, such as airlines, air charter operators, private aircraft operators, aviation training organisations, and air traffic management organisations, require that a safety-management system be instituted in the organisation to operate safely. There is a need to develop a safety culture throughout the organisation so that the goal of a safe operation can be achieved. This requires the acceptance of the concept by all in the organisation, from the top management to the staff on the floor. Everyone must buy in. This requires training and instilling in all staff the concept of operating safely.

In all sectors of the aviation industry, training is a critical component of carrying out the business. Staff must be trained and qualified in what they are doing. There is a need for the employment of experienced and skilled staff so that the maintenance of acceptable safety standards is achieved. In all cases, retraining or refresher training and practice with continuous testing is critical to a safe operation.

This book provides summaries of descriptions of the different sectors of the aviation industry to give readers a basic understanding of what aviation involves. This book may be just enough to give a reader an idea, or it may be just enough to trigger an underlying interest in pursuing a career in an aviation-related profession.

Happy reading!
Fred Mabonga

Table of Contents

Abbreviations

Abbreviation	Description
AMO	Aircraft maintenance organisation
AOC	Air operator certificate
ATC	Air traffic control
ATO	Approved training organisation
ATR	Avions Transport Régional (Italian-French aircraft manufacturer)
BAE	British Aerospace
CAA	Civil Aviation Authority
CAAC	Civil Aviation Authority of China
CASA	Civil Aviation Safety Authority (of Australia)
C of A	Certificate of Airworthiness
CRM	Crew resource management
DGCA	Directorate General of Civil Aviation
EASA	European Aviation Safety Agency
EADS	European Aeronautic Defence and Space Company
FAA	Federal Aviation Administration (of USA)
GMC	Ground movement control
GMP	Ground movement planning
IATA	International Air Transport Association
ICAN	International Commission for Air Navigation
ICAO	International Civil Aviation Organisation
IFR	Instrument flight rules
MAC	Mooney Airplane Company (of USA)
MCC	Maintenance control centre
PICAO	Provisional International Civil Aviation Organisation
SARPs	Standards and recommended practices
SMC	Surface movement control
SMGCS	Surface movement guidance and control systems
SMR	Surface movement radar
SSR	Secondary surveillance radar
TC	Transport Canada
TCAS	Traffic Collision Avoidance System

TWR	Tower
UHF	Ultra-high frequency
UAV	Unmanned air vehicle
VFR	Visual flight rules
VHF	Very high frequency

Chapter One

About Aviation

Aviation can be defined as the flying or operating of aircraft. It involves the design, development, production, operation, and use of aircraft. In the modern-day concept, aviation refers especially to heavier-than-air aircraft.

According to researchers aviation is derived from the word *avis*, the Latin word for *bird*. Aviation activities revolve around the aircraft. Aircraft is defined as an airplane, helicopter, or other machine capable of flight. Synonyms for aircraft include airplane, aeroplane, plane, and ship. These words are used in different parts of the world to refer to aircraft.

An aircraft is a machine that can fly by getting support from the air or atmosphere. It overcomes gravity by using static or dynamic lift of its structure or, in some cases, the downward thrust from jet engines.

Therefore, aviation refers to activity around aircraft. Aircraft are normally flown by pilots on board the aircraft. However, aircraft can also be unmanned and may be remotely controlled.

Aircraft operations are usually classified by their intended use. For example, aircraft may be classified for purposes of private use, aerial work, or public transport (passengers and cargo).

Chapter Two

Aviation History

Humans first achieved flight using hot air balloons. A scientist by the name of Jean-François Pilâtre de Rozier is believed to have launched the first hot air balloon in Paris, France, September 19, 1783. de Rozier was a French national. He was a teacher of chemistry and physics. This balloon was known as Aerostat Reveillon. In this balloon were a sheep, a duck, and a rooster. The balloon was in the air for fifteen minutes before crashing to the ground. de Rozier worked with another French national by the name of Marquis d'Arlandes to launch the first manned balloon on November 21, 1783. Two French brothers named Joseph and Etienne Montgolfier manufactured this balloon. de Rozier later died while attempting to cross the English Channel in a hot air balloon. He and his companion on that flight, Pierre Romian, were the first humans to die in an air crash.

The first people to successfully fly across the English Channel were Jean Pierre Blanchard, a French balloonist, and John Jefferies, his American co-pilot, in 1785. At the time, the English Channel was considered great distance to cover by flight, so this was a historical event.

A hot air balloon.

Fixed-wing aircraft

The story of the aviation industry as we know it today started at the beginning of the twentieth century. On December 17, 1903, the first powered, piloted aircraft took off.

Brothers Orville Wright and Wilbur Wright are credited with this first flight. The Wright brothers were inventors. They designed and built the aircraft that became known as The Flyer. Its main parts were the structure, motor, and propeller, and it weighed about 700 pounds (which is equivalent to about 320 kilograms).

To launch The Flyer, the Wright brothers built a movable downhill track to help the aircraft gain enough speed to take off. After two attempts, Orville Wright took The Flyer for a sustained, twelve-second flight December 17, 1903. With this, history was made. This was the first successful, powered, and piloted flight in history. The aircraft flew at a height of twenty feet and took place at Kitty Hawk, a beach in North Carolina, United States.

On November 9, 1904, the first flight lasting more than five minutes was achieved by Wilbur Wright in an aircraft known as The Flyer II.

The first assisted flight by the Wright brothers, December 17, 1903.

From here onwards, it became known that it was possible to build an aircraft and actually fly it. Many other inventors started to design and build aircraft. This aircraft-building trade spread across nations. Many different types of aircraft were built for various purposes, including air transportation for private use, air transportation for hire and reward, air ambulances for speedy transportation for medical purposes, aerial photography, aerial mapping, and weapons of war.

World War I (1914 to 1918)

World War I was fought mostly by soldiers in trenches. This was the first major war where airplanes were used. Balloons had been used for observation purposes, including artillery spotting, reconnaissance, and strategic bombing, in earlier wars. As aeroplanes were just coming into military use at the beginning of the war they were used mainly for reconnaissance. Pilots and engineers were learning on the job, and they later developed many specialised aircraft types, such as fighters, bombers and ground-attack aeroplanes.

Pilots were able to acquire specialised skills as fighter pilots. The impact of aircraft on the course of war was mainly tactical rather than strategic. Most importantly was the direct cooperation with ground forces, especially ranging and correcting artillery fire. The first signs of the strategic roles of aircraft in future wars became apparent at this time.

These events led to the rapid development of aviation industry with players from different parts of the world.

World War II (1939 to 1945)

By the time the Second World War started, the aircraft industry and aviation in general had developed dramatically in relation to the end of World War I.

The use of the aircraft as a weapon fuelled the technological development of the aircraft. The countries with air power were perceived to be much stronger militarily. This was due to the added advantage of being airborne and therefore higher than the firing power on the ground. The speed and agility of aircraft was also key.

The countries involved in the manufacture of aircraft invested resources in research and development and intensified the production of more advanced aircraft for both military and civil use.

New aircraft were developed to carry more passengers and travel at higher speeds for longer distances. The carriage of cargo by air became a faster way to transport trade goods and became an advantage for landlocked countries. Heavy loads were lifted by air for military and commercial civil purposes alike. Air transportation technology developed at a higher pace.

Modern aviation

After World War II, the aviation technology developed into other forms of research, eventually leading to the development of rockets and aerospace vehicles used for space exploration. Humans landed on the moon in 1969, just sixty-six years after the Wright brothers' first flight.

Other developments also included the jet engine and the helicopter. Helicopters have greater agility with the ability to perform vertical take-offs and landings as well as hover.

Helicopters now perform many civil and military roles. They are able to hover, fly backwards and sideways, and perform other desirable manoeuvres. Helicopters are also known as rotary wing aircraft or choppers. The aeroplane is also known as the fixed wing aircraft.

Fixed wing jet aircraft were also designed to be able to hover, fly backwards and sideways, and perform other desirable manoeuvres mainly for military purposes.

The 1980s saw further development of aviation, and manufacturers in the United States and Europe were competing to develop more advanced aircraft and aviation support systems such as air traffic management systems.

The 1990s and the early part of the twenty-first century saw further development of modern aviation, making air transportation a highly technical and efficient business. This development included the design and production of unmanned air vehicles (UAV), which are remotely piloted aircraft. These are utilised for both civil and military purposes.

Another aircraft designed after World War II was the reusable space shuttle. It is able to take off vertically using rocket launchers. It is then able to land back on earth as a conventional aircraft would.

By the twenty-first century, the major aircraft manufacturers were located in the United States, Europe, Russia, Brazil, and China.

By 2011, the largest passenger aircraft was the Airbus A380. It is a double-decker, wide-body, four-engine jet aircraft manufactured by the European corporation Airbus, a subsidiary of EADS. This aircraft is assembled in Toulouse, France. This aircraft can carry up to 555 passengers.

A typical operational seating is 525 passengers in three classes. The aircraft is capable of flying 8,500 nautical miles or 15,700 kilometres nonstop, carrying more people at a lower cost and with less impact on the environment than preceding aircraft types.

A320 one of the aircraft types manufactured by Airbus

The largest cargo aircraft in the world is the Antonov An-225 Mriya. It was designed by the Soviet Union in the 1980s. It has six jet engines, and with a gross weight of 640 tonnes, it is the heaviest aircraft ever manufactured. It is also the biggest in size by length and wingspan. It holds the world's record for airlifted payloads at 189,980 kilograms.

Antonov An-124 is one of the heavy cargo aircraft manufactured in Russia.

Very light aircraft known as micro-lights are used for Hang-gliding: A form of aviation recreation and also used for sight-seeing

General aviation light aircraft operations: These are light aircraft used for short distance flights and training

Chapter Three

Aviation Regulations

In the early days of flying, there were no regulations governing the operation of aircraft. Anyone could build an aircraft and fly it without any input from any controlling authority.

By the 1940s, many aircraft were in operation all over the world. Many were in civil operations and the military. Others were private operators for personal business and pleasure.

As aircraft developed and more players got involved in the manufacture and operation thereof, incidents and accidents increased. Aircraft could collide mid-air, crash to the ground, and cause damage to property as well as death.

As the incidents and accidents involving aircraft increased, there was alarm among the residents of the countries involved in the manufacture and operation of aircraft. There had to be some control or order to the way aircraft were operated. Regulations governing the operation of aircraft were necessary

Since the aircraft operation went beyond national borders in various countries' air space, there had to be some form of control involving several countries.

The major countries that operated most aircraft in the world decided to have a meeting to decide how to develop the control of aircraft movement.

Before the Second World War, the control of aviation was achieved through the Paris Convention of 1919. Its governing body was called the International Commission for Air Navigation (ICAN). At this point in time, there were only fifty sovereign states in the world; ICAN included thirty-three of these states. The next organised control was during the Havana Convention of 1928. The Havana Convention was ratified by only eleven states.

During the Second World War, the technological advancement of aviation was very significant. Its use developed the technical and operational possibilities for air transport the world over. Significantly large numbers of people and goods were transported over long distances. Infrastructure to support these operations was also developed.

By 1942, it was already apparent that civil air transportation was going to be critical in international relations after the war. There were already discussions in Canada to form an international civil aviation control mechanism.

The Quebec Conference was held in Quebec City in Canada from August 10 to 14, 1943. It was hosted by Canada's prime minister at the time, William Lyon Mackenzie King; Franklin Roosevelt and Winston Churchill both attended. Post-war aviation policy was discussed, as was the need to form an international organisation to handle international civil aviation. It became apparent that after the war the aviation industry would play a major role in the peace that would follow.

On September 11, 1944, the United States extended an invitation to fifty-three governments for an international civil aviation conference to be convened in Chicago in November 1944 to make arrangements for the immediate establishment of provisional world air routes and services. It was also to set up an interim council to collect, record, and study data concerning international aviation and to make recommendations for its improvement.

The most important result of the conference was the drawing up of a convention on international civil aviation. This became known as the Chicago Convention, the original text of which was in English, French, and Spanish. This became the charter of a new body established to guide and develop international civil aviation.

On December 7, 1944, the conference concluded with the signature of a final act that was a formal and official record summarizing the work.

The organisation was named the Provisional International Civil Aviation Organization (PICAO). It was established by the Chicago Conference, as an interim body pending the ratification of a permanent world civil aviation convention. Canada was selected to host the headquarters. The Canadian government chose Montreal for PICAO's headquarters, as it was at that time the leading metropolis of the country; it was also the main hub for international civil air transport.

PICAO later became the International Civil Aviation Organisation (ICAO). ICAO is now an aviation agency of the United Nations.

The aims and objectives of ICAO are stated in the Chicago Convention. They are to foster the planning and development of international air transport so as to ensure the safe and orderly growth of international civil aviation throughout the world.

Therefore, with the birth of ICAO, it became possible to control aviation.

ICAO

ICAO seeks to encourage the art of aircraft design and operation for peaceful purposes; encourage the development of airways, airports, and air navigation facilities for international civil aviation; meet the needs of the people of the world for safe, regular, efficient, and economical air transport; prevent economic waste caused by unreasonable competition; ensure that the rights of contracting states are fully respected and that every contracting state has a fair opportunity to operate international airlines; avoid discrimination between contracting states; promote safety of flight in international air navigation; and generally promote the development of all aspects of international civil aeronautics.

By 2011, ICAO had 191 member states throughout the world. They are also known as contracting states.

Each state establishes and operates a state civil aviation authority (CAA). The CAA uses the ICAO standards and recommended practices (SARPs). Each state CAA develops the national aviation regulations based on the SARPs as the minimum standard and are adapted to the local operating environment.

New developments in aviation regulation issues governing aviation are disseminated to the aviation industry. ICAO continuously researches and disseminates any new information to the industry through the member states CAAs. These documents are known as annexes to the convention.

Chapter Four

Aircraft Manufacture

Aircraft manufacturing has come a long way since the days of the Wright brothers, who were themselves inventors, manufacturers, pilots, and aircraft-maintenance engineers.

An aircraft manufacturer is as a company or individual involved in the various aspects of designing, building, testing, selling, and maintaining aircraft and aircraft parts.

Aircraft manufacturing falls under the aerospace industry. Aerospace is a high technology industry and includes designing, building, testing, selling, and maintaining missiles, rockets, and/or spacecraft.

To make an aircraft, the manufacturers have to source a number of parts to be able to construct the aircraft. There is a large network of specialized parts manufacturers and suppliers throughout the world that support the requirements of these manufacturers.

Aeroplanes used by airlines for commercial operations for passengers or cargo are also known as airliners. These are medium to large aircraft.

General aviation aircraft are usually smaller aircraft than airliners. General aviation includes all nonscheduled civil flying, both private and commercial. General aviation can also include business flights, private aviation, flight training, air charter, ballooning, parachuting, aerial photography, hang-gliding, gliding, foot-launched powered hang-gliders, air ambulances, crop dusting, charter flights, traffic reporting, police air patrols, and forest fire fighting.

So much has changed in aviation since the 1944 Convention on International Civil aviation. There have been technological developments and regulatory changes aimed at the improvement of aviation safety.

In modern aviation, the aircraft manufacturing industry is strictly regulated by the civil aviation authority (CAA) of the state where the manufacturing takes place, also known as the state of manufacture. This regulation includes the manufacture of parts and accessories that go into the manufacture of an aircraft, covering outsourced and contracted work.

In regulating the manufacturers, the CAAs follow the ICAO standards and recommended practices. This is because ICAO is committed to encourage the art of aircraft design and operation.

The aircraft manufacturing process involves complying with the following:

- The facility must be approved by the state CAA as suitable for the manufacture of aircraft. The process of approval includes demonstration to the CAA of the capability of the facility to manufacture aircraft in accordance with procedures, rules, and processes.
- The manufacturing facility is approved for each particular type of aircraft that is to be manufactured there.
- For each aircraft type, the initial design, also known as the prototype, is required to be approved by the state CAA.
- For each aircraft type, the manufacturing process is to be approved by the state CAA.
- For the prototype, the state CAA has to approve the initial test flight and certification issued for the type.
- Any subsequent modifications to the type are to be approved by the state CAA.
- To maintain the approval, the manufacturer is subjected to routine audits by the state
- CAA.

There are several aircraft manufacturers in world. Again, aircraft manufacturers are found in Brazil, Canada, China, the European Union, Russia, and the United States.

The major aircraft manufacturers are Airbus Industries in Europe and Boeing in the United States. By 2012, the largest Boeing passenger aircraft was the Boeing B747-400. By 2012, the largest passenger aircraft made by Airbus was the Airbus A380. In 2012, the Airbus A380 was the largest passenger aircraft in the world.

There is concerted competition between Airbus and Boeing for the sale of their aircraft types worldwide. They do compete for market share in sales all over the world.

Most aircraft manufacturers build aircraft for carriage of both passengers and cargo.

Within the European Union, aerospace companies such as EADS, BAE Systems, Thales, Dassault, Saab, and Finmeccanica account for a large share of the global aerospace industry and research effort including the manufacture of aircraft and aviation equipment.

In Russia, there are two large aerospace companies (United Aircraft Building Corporation [encompassing Mikoyan, Sukhoi, Ilyushin, Tupolev, Yakovlev, and Irkut] and Oboronprom) among the world leaders in the aerospace manufacturing industry.

In the United States, aside from Boeing, the leading manufacturers are United Technologies Corporation and Lockheed Martin. They are also among the most widely known aerospace manufacturers in the world.

The major locations where the civil aerospace industry facilities are worldwide include:

- Boeing: Seattle, Daytona Beach, and St Louis in the United States
- Bombardier: Montreal, Canada
- Airbus/EADS/ATR: Toulouse, France, and Hamburg, Germany
- BAE Systems, Airbus, and AgustaWestland: the northwest of England and Bristol, United Kingdom
- Embraer: Brazil
- Komsomolsk-on-Amur and Irkutsk: Russia.

Airbus, Boeing, and Tupolev mainly manufacturer the wide-body and narrow-body jet airliners, while Bombardier and Embraer concentrate on regional airliners.

The major manufacturers of medium to large civil transport aircraft are Airbus, Boeing, Bombardier, Embraer, and Tupolev.

Airbus: Airbus is one of the world's leading aircraft manufacturers, fulfilling about half or more of the orders for airliners with more than 100 seats. Airbus is based in Europe with its headquarters in Toulouse, France, and operated twelve sites in Europe, including France, Germany, Spain, and the UK by 2009.

A modern aircraft cockpit layout and displays

Boeing: Boeing is one of the other main aerospace companies and is the largest manufacturer of commercial jetliners and military aircraft combined.

Bombardier: Bombardier has its headquarters are in Montréal, Canada. Bombardier Aerospace is the world's third largest civil aircraft manufacturer and is a leader in the design and manufacture of innovative aviation products and services for the business, regional, and amphibious aircraft markets.

Embraer: Embraer is based in São José dos Campos, Brazil. It one of the main aircraft manufacturers in the world and focuses on specific market segments with high growth potential in commercial, defence, and executive aviation.

Tupolev: Tupolev is a Russian aerospace and defence company headquartered in Moscow, Russia. Tupolev develops, manufactures, and overhauls both civil and military aerospace products such as aircraft and weapons systems. It also actively develops missile and naval aviation technologies.

Some of the manufacturers of small aircraft that serve the general aviation market with a focus on private aviation and flight training are Cessna, Cirrus Design, Diamond, Mooney, and Piper.

Cessna: Cessna Aircraft Company is one of the leading designer and manufacturer of light and midsize business jets, utility turboprops, and single engine aircraft. It is based in Wichita, Kansas, and it has been making aircraft for more than eighty years.

Cirrus Design: Cirrus Design Corporation is based in the United States and has been an aircraft manufacturer of single-engine, piston-powered aircraft since 1984. Its best-selling model in its class has been the SR22.

Diamond: Diamond Aircraft Industries is an Austrian-based manufacturer of general aviation aircraft, motor gliders, and simulators. It is a global manufacturer with offices in North America, Europe, Asia, and Australia. It produces aircraft for flight schools and private operators.

Mooney: Founded in 1929, the Mooney Airplane Company (MAC) is an American-based manufacturer of single-engine general aviation aircraft.

Piper: Piper Aircraft is a manufacturer of general aviation aircraft, located at the Vero Beach Municipal Airport in Vero Beach, Florida. Mr William T. Piper introduced the Piper Cub in 1937, and since then, Piper Aircraft has become the only general aviation manufacturer to offer a complete line of aircraft. It includes rugged trainers, high-performance turbo props, and the new Piper Jet.

China Aviation Industry Corporation: This is the manufacturer in China. It makes the Xian MA60, which is a turbo prop-powered commercial aircraft. It is developed from the popular Russian regional aircraft Antonov An-24 and is equipped with modern power plant (engines), equipment, and design concept. It is suitable for short- and medium-haul commuter service. It is powered by Pratt & Whitney PWC 127 J (Canada) engines with Hamilton Propellers (United States), and most of its avionics are made in the United States. The APU, environment control system, and many other systems are also made in the United States. The first MA60s commenced operations in 2004. An updated version is known as the MA600, and it made its maiden flight in September 2008. The aircraft is equipped with new avionics, passenger cabins, and engines with increased thrust.

Chapter Five

Aircraft Maintenance

Aircraft maintenance is a highly specialised skill, requiring extensive specialised training and experience before maintenance personnel can be allowed to certify to release an aircraft for flight.

With regard to aircraft maintenance processes, ICAO plays a critical role in setting the standards and recommended practices. The state CAAs also play an important role in the oversight of the state's maintenance facilities.

To function satisfactorily, a maintenance facility must be approved by the state CAA. The facility is then known as the approved maintenance organisation (AMO). An AMO is issued with an AMO licence by the CAA once the CAA is satisfied that the AMO meets the prescribed standards.

The AMO must have adequate tools and equipment to carry out the maintenance on the aircraft types they are approved to maintain. The type of work carried out may include modifications, inspections, repairs (defect rectification), parts replacements, and overhauls.

In addition, they must have adequate maintenance personnel for the volume of work to be carried out. The maintenance personnel must be adequately trained and experienced on the work they are to carry out. The state CAA carries out routine oversight audits to ensure compliance with the regulations.

Aircraft maintenance engineers are trained to a standard and syllabus determined by the state CAA as guided by ICAO annexes. The training facility for maintenance engineers is approved by the state CAA and is known as approved training organisation (ATO). The pass mark is set at seventy-five percent. In some subjects, it is at eighty-five percent. This is because in aircraft maintenance personnel cannot afford to make mistakes. On successful completion of the training, an aircraft maintenance engineer's licence is issued to the candidate, who then becomes a licensed aircraft maintenance engineer. The final examination for issuance of the licence is carried out by the state CAA and includes the written and oral examinations.

The licensed aircraft engineer is charged with the responsibility of releasing the aircraft to service after maintenance work is carried out on the aircraft. This is done by issuing a certificate of release to service with the engineer's signature and licence number on it.

The aircraft is then ready for flight.

Aircraft maintenance is described as the overhaul, repair, inspection, or modification of an aircraft or aircraft component. Maintenance includes the installation or removal of a component from an aircraft or aircraft subassembly. Maintenance may include such tasks as ensuring compliance with airworthiness directives or service bulletins.

Aircraft maintenance regulation

Aircraft maintenance is highly regulated. The regulation is carried out by airworthiness authorities. There are various airworthiness authorities around the world. The major airworthiness authorities include:

- Civil Aviation Administration of China (CAAC), China
- Civil Aviation Safety Authority (CASA), Australia
- Directorate General of Civil Aviation (DGCA), India
- European Aviation Safety Agency (EASA), Europe
- Federal Aviation Administration (FAA), United States
- Transport Canada (TC), Canada

Airworthiness release

After the completion of any maintenance task, the engineer authorized by the national airworthiness authority signs a release document stating that maintenance has been performed in accordance with the applicable airworthiness requirements. The professional authorised to sign this release document is an appropriately qualified licensed aircraft maintenance engineer. The release document will carry the engineer's signature and licence number. This is important for traceability purposes.

Aircraft maintenance hangar

In an aviation organisation, it is commonly recognised that the cost of aircraft maintenance ranks as one of the highest expenditure items, if not the highest. However, the finance authorities in organisations with good safety records have long realised that the cost of aircraft maintenance is imperative.

Aircraft engineering categories

Aircraft engineers can specialise in following categories:

- Engines and airframe

- Avionics (this term derives from the phrase *aviation electronics*)

Engines and airframe specialists are experts in the maintenance of aircraft engines and the aircraft structures including wings, landing gear, and control surfaces.

Avionics specialists are experts in aircraft electronic systems such systems as radio communication, radio navigation, weather radar, instruments, and electrical.

Avionics workshop

Chapter Six

Aircraft Operations

In the aircraft industry, flight operation normally refers to the activity of actually flying the aircraft and involves planning, putting in action schedules, and knowing the exact location of aircraft at all times.

The aircraft operator normally has a control centre equipped with radio communication in order to maintain contact with aircraft.

The key personnel to aircraft operation are the pilots. The pilots are trained to high levels of competence and safety. In all operations, the critical function centres on safety. Pilots accept aircraft from aircraft maintenance engineers after carrying out their own professional pilot inspections and tests. This acceptance by the pilot is in the form of signing a technical logbook once the pilot is satisfied that the aircraft is in airworthy condition as per specifications and regulations. Therefore, through the technical logbook, the aircraft maintenance engineers attest that the aircraft is in airworthy condition. The pilot signs that, after his/her inspection and tests, the aircraft is airworthy.

Aircraft operators do have a flight operations centre from where they control all aircraft movement. This control includes flight and cabin crew roster management. Flight operations centres can also manage flight planning, including route planning, and obtain weather reports along the planned routes. The planning can include obtaining over-flight and landing clearance for various destinations.

The flight operations centre monitors aircraft movement at all times. The personnel who work in the flight operations centre are known as aircraft dispatchers. Aircraft dispatchers are responsible for planning a successful flight. This centre is where pilots and cabin crew report for work and sign in. Most airlines do have standby crews in case of personnel who do not show due to sickness or other reasons.

Some airlines do have a maintenance control centre (MCC). This MCC complements the flight operations centre. The personnel who work in the MCC are experienced aircraft engineers and are in regular contact with the flight crew by radio and other means in case of technical difficulties. The flight crews consult MCC on technical matters as necessary.

Therefore, MCC manages the technical condition of all aircraft in the airline fleet. It gives technical support to cockpit crews in case of technical defects at all times the airline fleet is in operation. Initiation, control, and coordination of all actions necessary to solve technical malfunctions at line stations in conjunction with the airline's flight operations control centre. They initiate, control, and coordinate technical field team assistance in the cases of out-of-base technical difficulties. They maintain a database for all technical delays and deferred defects for reference. They produce daily technical reports.

Therefore, for flight-operation success, there are aircraft dispatchers, flight crews (pilots), and cabin crews. Then there is the MCC. At all times, all these professionals are working as a team to ensure that all flights for the airline are going smoothly. Teamwork is necessary.

System safety

Safety management is an important element of an aviation organisation.

It is important for an aircraft operator to institute a safety management system in order to ensure all operations are carried our safely. This is the same as risk management of all aircraft operations, and it covers procedures in case of an incident or accident.

An effective safety-management system should apply throughout the organisation.

The safety-management system framework has four components:

- Safety policy and objectives
- Safety risk management
- Safety assurance
- Safety promotion

The aircraft operators' management must maintain the highest standards of excellence in operations and business conduct in full compliance with aviation regulatory requirements. They must be committed to ensure a proactive safety program is in place and does not compromise safety commitment. The management should be committed to ensure that regular audits are conducted internally and that all staff members participate in the process.

There must be a system to evaluate the level of safety in the organisation.

Airport terminal building

Helicopter operations base

Chapter Seven

The Airline Business

The airline business can be defined as the carriage of passengers and/or goods (freight) from one place to another for hire and reward. It is therefore a commercial operation.

It can also be said that aviation business is not about selling transportation. People can transport themselves on foot or by boat. The aviation or airline business more than anything else is about the selling of time. That means that speed counts for a lot in air transportation.

When properly planned and implemented, the airline business can be a profitable business. It is important to do a feasibility study to determine the viability of the airline business for a specific region of operation. Even in consideration of the current number of airlines in the world, there is still a ready market for starting a new airline, provided an appropriate model is selected. Such opportunities exist in many developing countries in emerging markets.

For example, air traffic continues to grow globally. Particularly in Africa, the growth has been sustained over the last five to six years. This means that air transportation is attracting more customers each year. According to the ICAO report of 2011, this growth has been sustained in the period from 2005 to 2010. Africa has about fifty four countries and a population of a billion people. The infrastructure for surface connectivity between African countries is very poor. This fact is an opportunity for the development of an efficient air transportation system that can connect African countries. The need for connectivity is ever present. This need is evidenced by the need for movement of goods for business and the movement of people for business travel and tourism. It is evident that due to the existing demand for intra Africa trade air transportation is the quickest solution that can be implemented in a timeous manner. Air transportation has benefits over land transportation. Africa is a very large continent. Another fact is that there is a unanimous political will among African countries to connect all the African countries for the purposes of business and tourism travel. The most optimum way to achieve this goal is through air transportation.

The threats to profitability include effects such as restrictions and taxes as well as the cost of labour and the comparison with other regions of the world. There is need for a conducive regulatory and policy environment to complement the African airline business and lead to profitability. Africa is becoming increasingly attractive to foreign investors, and this phenomenon can lead to an air traffic increase.

The concept of the low-cost carriers (LCC) can contribute to increasing connectivity among African countries. Good business sense can lead to profitability. This concept will allow more people to afford air travel.

For a landlocked country, as many African countries are, the airline industry is of strategic importance. This mode of air transportation guarantees an alternative gateway to the rest of the world, and it is the only means that can facilitate the movement of people and goods to various destinations overseas without having to pass through another country.

It must be stated that Africa accounts for only three percent of the global air traffic. Therefore, there is a lot of room for growth.

When operating an airline, it is critical to adhere to safety procedures and regulations. The airline business operates under the functioning principles of the aviation industry. The aviation industry is one of the most regulated industries in the world.

When operating an airline, it is advisable to join the International Air Transport Association (IATA). IATA is an international industry trade group of airlines. It functions to represent, lead, and serve the airline industry. IATA represents more than eighty percent of scheduled international air traffic. All airline rules and regulations are defined by IATA. The main aim of IATA is to provide safe and secure transportation to its passengers.

IATA has regional offices throughout the world.

Therefore, the foregoing do illustrate that the mechanisms are there in place. When utilized, the mechanisms can make the airline business safe.

Noncompliance with the rules and procedures can lead to unsafe operating conditions. Unsafe conditions can lead to customers avoiding using the service and therefore leading to business losses. This demonstrates how sustaining a high safety standard makes good business sense. Unsafe operating conditions can also lead to incidents and accidents, which is bad for business. Reference can be made to regularly published IATA and ICAO statistics. An appropriate business plan can enhance both safety and good business practices all in one entity. It is advisable to institute in the airline business safety practices in accordance with international standards.

A major issue in air transportation is safety. There is a requirement for safe take-offs and landings day after day. This also makes good business sense. Customers are looking for safe and reliable airlines for their air transportation needs (including passenger and cargo).

The safety requirement in the airline business cannot be overemphasised. It is repeatedly instilled in the airline staff in performance of their duties. In fact, the core of a well-managed aviation organisation centres on its safety procedures program. This is in addition to the business requirement for excellent customer service, staff development, aircraft fleet renewal, and route growth that go with operating a successful airline.

The achievement of safety standards and safety goals or targets depends largely on the plan and the training of personnel and then putting into practice the safety program. The achievement of a good safety record can add to good reputation, and for those companies in commercial operations, it leads to increased business as your customers become aware that they are safe in your hands. This means you put safety considerations first.

The way to achieve a total safety concept in an airline begins with the training of personnel to ensure compliance with the organisation's safety program and aviation regulations.

It is therefore reasonable to argue that training and implementation of safety program are critical in operating an aviation business.

An airline can be defined as a commercial enterprise that provides scheduled flights for passengers. An airline also provides air transport services for traveling passengers and freight (cargo).

Airlines may lease or own their aircraft with which to supply these services and may form partnerships or alliances with other airlines for mutual benefit.

Generally, airline companies are certified with an air operator certificate (AOC) or license issued by a state CAA before they can be able to commence business. The conditions for issuance of the AOC are designed in such a manner that the airline has to prove compliance with procedures and regulations with an emphasis on aviation safety.

There are different types of airlines and can vary from those operating a single aircraft carrying mail or cargo, to the large international airlines operating hundreds of aircraft. Airline services can be categorized as being intercontinental, intracontinental, domestic, regional, or international and may be operated as scheduled services or charters.

To operate the airline as a viable business, the owner may wish to evaluate some operating factors with the following as examples:

- Direct costs, fixed costs, and annual budget data
- Aircraft operating costs
- Evaluate aircraft performance data
- Staff remuneration
- Airport charges such as landing fees, parking fees, and over-flight fees
- International currency rates fluctuations
- Aircraft type selection to meet operating business purposes

Chapter Eight

Training

In the aviation industry, training is governed by strict regulations. The professionals in the industry must go through rigorous training and testing before they can become qualified aviation professionals.

Most notable professions in aviation can be listed as pilots, aircraft engineers, cabin crew, and air traffic controllers.

There are other aviation professionals who make the aviation industry what it is. These other professionals include air navigation systems and communications engineers, flight/aircraft dispatchers, aviation meteorologists, airfield maintenance technical personnel, and other support professions that make up the teams that facilitates the safe operation of air transportation.

To achieve an efficient air transportation system, there has to be an input of training. The training for aviation professionals is thorough and recognises that there should not be much room for error. In all the training courses, the pass mark is set between seventy percent and eighty-five percent.

The training institutions have to be approved by the state CAAs. They follow very strict standards set by ICAO. Each approved training facility operates as an approved training organisation (ATO).

Due to the stringent emphasis on safety, highly skilled trainers and training equipment tends to be very costly. In all the training, aviation safety is emphasised.

The achievement of any safety goals starts with training. In fact, there is a popular saying in aviation that if you think training is expensive, try an accident.

There are several training institutions for aviation professions all across the world in various countries.

IATA provides aviation training to the aviation industry. It has professional development programs and training aviation professionals to achieve safety, security, and sustainability. This is carried out in accordance with international standards and industry regulations.

ICAO has an official training directory, which has a comprehensive list of approved aviation-training providers. This enables prospective students to access the information regarding training providers on its website. It lists more than 700 training centres in 100 countries.

ICAO encourages training stakeholders to visit its website; www.icao.int for information on the aviation training community.

Training approval

It is very important for aviation training institutions to be approved by civil aviation authorities. This means that they have been audited and found to be in compliance with all the regulatory requirements. Civil aviation authorities have a training policy that stipulates the approval and licensing of training organizations and training courses. They will audit and inspect the facilities before any approval or licensing is issued to the training organisation. Therefore, they must be satisfied that the training organisation and courses fully meet the standards and methodological requirements, including objectives of competency and performance-based training processes.

The civil aviation training policy addresses all areas of aviation safety and security. The civil aviation training policy enables the implementation of a comprehensive framework to ensure that all training provided by approved training organisations is assessed to ensure that it meets vigorous standards for the design and development of training courses.

The civil aviation training includes the use of technology for simulation of flight situations for the purpose of training pilots, aircraft engineers, air traffic controllers, and cabin crews.

Approved training organisations are periodically reassessed to renew their approval or license. In some countries, this is annually. In others, it is every two years. It all depends on the current national aviation regulations. Training organisations seeking new approval or licence of training activities are responsible for developing and/or offering courses that fully meet the regulatory standards and methodological requirements.

Approved training organisations also offer recurrent training for aviation professionals. These are short refresher courses to ensure continued competence.

Whereas the civil aviation authorities issue approvals and licences to training organisations that meet the regulatory requirements, they also reserve the right to withdraw approval or licences of any approved training organisation that fails to meet those regulatory requirements.

The civil aviation authority approval or licence indicates that the delivered training programs, facilities, and instructors meet the criteria of quality and relevance needed to ensure that the skills and knowledge necessary to implement regulatory requirements are provided. It also indicates that training programs, facilities, and instructors are managed in such a way as to effectively support learning in accordance with the regulatory requirements.

The civil aviation authorities carry out oversight regarding the training and testing. The approved training organisation is responsible for fully meeting the regulatory requirements. However, the civil aviation authority periodically carries out inspections and audits to ensure continued compliance.

The approval or licence is granted or renewed only after an assessment conducted by the civil aviation authority confirms that regulatory requirements have been met.

A training session

Chapter Nine

Air Traffic Control

The movement of aircraft between airports within a country or across countries is carried out under the direct control of aviation professionals known as air traffic controllers.

Air traffic control (ATC) is a much specialised profession. Air traffic controllers go through rigorous professional training at approved training organisations.

An airfield is equipped with a control tower and hangars as well as accommodations for passengers and cargo. The airfield is also known as the aerodrome or airport.

An ATC tower is at an airfield from which air traffic is controlled by radio and observed physically and via radar.

International Civil Aviation Organisation (ICAO) requirements stipulate that ATC operations be conducted either in English or the language used by the station on the ground. In practice, the native language for a region is normally used; however, English must be used upon request.

Before embarking on a flight, the pilot in charge of the flight must file a flight plan with ATC. A flight plan is a form filled out by pilots used for navigational reference. It may include navigational structures on the ground as well as coordinates.

Therefore, ATC is a service provided by ground-based controllers who direct aircraft on the ground and through controlled airspace. The primary purpose of ATC systems worldwide is to prevent collisions, organise and expedite the flow of traffic, and provide information and other support for pilots when able. In some countries, ATC plays a security or defensive role or is operated by the military.

To prevent collisions, ATC enforces traffic separation rules, which ensures that each aircraft maintains a minimum amount of empty space around it at all times. Many aircraft also have collision-avoidance systems that provide additional safety by warning pilots when other planes get too close. These systems are known as traffic collision avoidance systems (TCAS) and are installed on board the aircraft. In some countries, an aircraft is not permitted to enter its airspace unless equipped with TCAS. This requirement is a safety measure.

In many countries, ATC provides services to all private, military, and commercial aircraft operating within its airspace. Depending on the type of flight being conducted and the airspace, ATC may issue instructions that pilots are required to obey. These can be verbal or written and are known as flight information.

An air traffic control tower

In many countries, the pilot in command of the flight is the final authority for the safe operation of the aircraft. The pilot may, in an emergency situation, deviate from ATC instructions to the extent required to deal with the situation. This is carried as the pilot's best professional consideration in view of the current emergency situation. In some instances, it could be a split-second decision for the safety of the passengers and crew.

The primary method of controlling the immediate airport environment is visual observation from the aerodrome control tower (TWR). The TWR is a tall, windowed structure located on the airport grounds. Aerodrome or tower controllers are responsible for the separation and efficient movement of aircraft and vehicles operating on the taxiways and runways of the airport itself, and aircraft in the air near the airport, generally up to twenty kilometres depending on the airport procedures.

Radar displays are also available to controllers at some airports. Controllers may use a radar system called secondary surveillance radar (SSR) for airborne traffic approaching and departing. These displays include a map of the area; the position of various aircraft; and data tags that include aircraft identification, speed, altitude, and other relevant information applicable to the aircraft. In adverse weather conditions, the tower controllers may also use surface movement radar (SMR), surface movement guidance and control systems (SMGCS), or advanced SMGCS to control traffic on the manoeuvring area (taxiways and runways).

The areas of responsibility for TWR controllers fall into three general operational disciplines: local control or air control, ground control, and flight data/clearance delivery. Other categories, such as apron control or ground movement planner, may exist at extremely busy airports.

Remote and virtual tower (RVT) is a system based on air traffic controllers being located somewhere other than at the local airport tower and still able to provide air traffic control services. Displays for the air traffic controllers may be either optical live video and/or synthetic images based on surveillance sensor data.

Ground control (sometimes known as ground movement control [GMC] or surface movement control [SMC]) is responsible for the airport movement areas as well as areas not released to the airlines or other users. This generally includes all taxiways, inactive runways, holding areas, and some transitional aprons or intersections where aircraft arrive, having vacated the runway or departure gate. Exact areas and control responsibilities are clearly defined in local documents and agreements at each airport. Any aircraft, vehicle, or person walking or working in these areas is required to have clearance from ground control. This is normally done via VHF/UHF radio, but there may be special cases where other processes are used. Most aircraft and airside vehicles have radios. Aircraft or vehicles without radios must respond to ATC instructions via aviation light signals or else be led by vehicles with radios. People working at the airport normally have a communications link through which they can communicate with ground control, commonly either by handheld radio or even cell phone. Ground control is vital to the smooth operation of the airport. This position impacts the sequencing of departure aircraft, affecting the safety and efficiency of airport operations.

Some busier airports have surface movement radar (SMR) designed to display aircraft and vehicles on the ground. These are used by ground control as an additional tool to control ground traffic, particularly at night or in poor visibility.

Local control (known to pilots as *tower* or *tower control*) is responsible for the active runway surfaces. Local control clears aircraft for take-off or landing, ensuring that prescribed runway separation will exist at all times. If local control detects any unsafe condition, a landing aircraft may be told to go around and be resequenced into the landing pattern by the approach or terminal area controller.

Within the TWR, a highly disciplined communications process between local control and ground control is an absolute necessity. Ground control must request and gain approval from local control to cross any active runway with any aircraft or vehicle. Likewise, local control must ensure that ground control is aware of any operations that will impact the taxiways and work with the approach radar controllers to create holes or gaps in the arrival traffic. This allows taxiing traffic to cross runways and departing aircraft to take off. Crew resource management (CRM) procedures are often used to ensure this communication process is efficient and clear.

ATC issues route clearances to aircraft, typically before they commence taxiing. These contain details of the route that the aircraft is expected to fly after departure. When weather or extremely high demand for a certain airport or airspace becomes a factor, there may be ground departure delays or the aircraft may be instructed to hold before landing.

ATC also controls aircraft push backs and engine starts, in which case it is known as ground movement planning (GMP). This is particularly important at heavily congested airports to prevent taxiway and apron conflict.

ATC ensures that pilots have the most current information regarding pertinent weather changes and airport ground delays, runway closures, and more.

With regard to air traffic flows, ATC is generally divided into departures, arrivals, and over flights. As aircraft move in and out of the terminal airspace, they are handed off to the next appropriate control facility (a control tower, an en route control facility, or a bordering terminal or approach control). Terminal control is responsible for ensuring that aircraft are at an appropriate altitude when they are handed off and that aircraft arrive at a suitable rate for landing.

ATC provides services to aircraft in flight between airports as well. Pilots fly under one of two sets of rules for separation: visual flight rules (VFR) or instrument flight rules (IFR). Air traffic controllers have different responsibilities to aircraft operating under the different sets of rules. IFR flights are under positive control, and VFR pilots can request flight following, which provides traffic advisory services on a time permitting basis and may also provide assistance in avoiding areas of adverse weather and flight restrictions.

En-route air traffic controllers issue clearances and instructions for airborne aircraft, and pilots are required to comply with these instructions. En route controllers also provide air traffic control services to many smaller airports around the country of operation, including clearance off of the ground and clearance for approach to an airport. Controllers adhere to a set of separation standards that define the minimum distance allowed between aircraft. These distances vary depending on the equipment and procedures used in providing ATC services.

ATC is responsible for aircraft that is climbing to their requested altitude while ensuring that the aircraft is properly separated from all other aircraft in the immediate area. As an aircraft reaches the boundary of a particular country's ATC control, it is handed over to the next country's ATC.

The challenges faced by the air traffic control system are primarily related to the volume of air traffic demand placed on the system and weather. Several factors dictate the amount of traffic that can land at an airport in a given amount of time. Each landing aircraft must touch down, slow, and exit the runway before the next aircraft crosses the approach end of the runway. Some large airports have additional runways and can handle more aircraft.

Adverse weather (such as rain, ice, or snow) can be a major factor at airports and can cause delays. A major weather problem is thunderstorms, which can be a hazard to aircraft. Aircraft have to deviate around storms.

http://www.freeimages.com/photo/1197756

Inside an air traffic control tower

Air navigation services include navigation aids equipment installed on the ground. These aids transmit electromagnetic signals that are received by aircraft and computed to display information to the pilot. This information, together with other navigation instruments, is used by pilots to navigate the aircraft with regard to direction, distance, and altitude.

Chapter Ten

Aviation Meteorology

Meteorology is the science of knowing the weather changes and predicting the future pattern of weather. It can be defined as the scientific study of the atmosphere to predict the weather. The use of computer technology enhances weather forecasting.

Weather is a very critical factor in the operation of aircraft.

Adverse weather can reduce the capacity of the en route air traffic system by requiring more space per aircraft or by causing congestion as many aircraft try to move through a limited airspace area to avoid thunderstorms. Weather considerations occasionally cause delays to aircraft prior to their departure as routes are closed due to thunderstorms.

Meteorological phenomena are observable weather events that are active and explained by the science of meteorology. Those events are bound by the variables that exist in Earth's atmosphere, including temperature; air pressure; water vapour; the gradients and interactions of each variable; and how systems on local, regional, and global levels impact weather and climatology. This science is used to predict the weather, which is also known as a weather forecast. The professionals who forecast weather are meteorologists.

Aviation weather meteorologists play an important role in helping pilots navigate their flight routes. In conjunction with air traffic controllers, aviation weather meteorologists work around the clock to make sure pilots can get to their destination as safely and as smoothly as possible.

Some aviation weather meteorologists work for airlines, others work for private companies, while some are employed in government departments.

The study of meteorology is deep science in its own right. For the purposes of this book, we shall limit it to the effects of weather and the usage of weather forecasting.

In relation to aviation, the various weather exhibits are in the form of characters of the sky: sunshine; rain; and atmospheric phenomena such as winds, thunder, lightning, snow, floods, valleys, rivers, lakes, wells, and other sources of water.

Aviation meteorology deals with the impact of weather on air traffic control. It is important for air crews to understand the implications of weather on their flight plan as well as their aircraft. As part of flight planning, pilots need to know the weather along the route they plan to fly.

In the winter, the effects of ice on aircraft can result in thrust reduction, drag increases, lift lessening, and weight increases. The results are an increase in stall speed and a deterioration of aircraft performance. In extreme cases, ice can form very quickly on the aircraft wings and if not removed it can result in reduction of the lifting power. This can lead to aircraft accidents.

Therefore, the airports that are prone to icing conditions in the winter are equipped with de-icing equipment. This is the equipment that sprays a substance on the aircraft to remove the ice before flight. This substance is a fluid based on propylene glycol.

The weather brief is given to the pilots before they take off so that they have an idea of the weather along their route. The preflight weather brief is mainly used to show any major risks to the flight, such as from thunderstorms, icing, and turbulence.

Chapter Eleven

Conclusion

From the first flight in 1903 by the Wright brothers on to the modern flights of the twenty-first century, the aviation industry has developed much faster than most other industries. In just over 110 years, the advancement in aviation technology has been phenomenal. Being able to fly heavier-than-air machines as the Wright brothers managed to do, aviation technology has been developed and used to fly into outer space, putting man on the moon in 1969 with Apollo 11 spacecraft, putting satellites into orbit, making reusable shuttle flights into space possible, and eventually putting a permanent station in space for communications and research.

The development of aviation has made it possible to use the aircraft in various roles. Today, aircraft can be used for the carriage of people in large numbers from one point of departure to multiple destinations for purposes of business, pleasure, and tourism. The transportation of people by air is a multibillion dollar industry covering the whole world. Millions of people travel by air to and from these places every single day. Today, this is mostly taken for granted, but it is a good illustration of the importance of aviation in the modern world.

In some cases, air transportation is utilised by those who can afford it as a personal means of transport. In the corporate business world, an organisation may own an aircraft for the transportation of their employees to improve on the speed of doing business with an aim of making the organisation more efficient and more profitable than it would otherwise be.

Another aviation sector for those who can afford it is the recreation sector such as for air competitions and displays of skills.

The aircraft can also be used for the transportation of cargo/freight. This air cargo transportation is the main means of transporting perishable goods to distant destinations across the world. An example is the business of the export of fresh flowers from Africa to Europe. This is made possible by air transportation in order to reach a destination while still fresh. Other perishables transported over long distances by air include fresh fruit, vegetables, and fish.

Another role of aviation in the modern world is the agriculture crop dusting. In this role, light aircraft are used to fly at very low altitudes to spray fields of crops with agricultural chemicals. This is much faster than doing it on the ground by hand.

Aircraft are also used in aerial surveys flights for mapping to aid in determining the local area map of a specific place. The aircraft can also be used for exploration of minerals using airborne equipment that can detect minerals underground.

Aviation is also used in medical support by utilising appropriate aircraft to deliver medicines and medical supplies to remote parts where surface transportation is either difficult or nonexistent. In addition, the aircraft can also be used in emergency evacuation from remote places to destinations where appropriate medical treatment can be accessed. Medical evacuation can also be used in cities where it is critical for the injured person to receive medical treatment as soon as possible. In these cases, the type of aircraft most frequently used is the helicopter as it can land at places a fixed wing aircraft (aeroplane) cannot. The aircraft used for medical evacuation is a specially equipped aircraft with all the necessary emergency medical equipment on board in order that the patient is in good care and accompanied by medical personnel on board.

Another role the aircraft can play is in the search and rescue missions where there has been an accident on the surface, ground, or water where it is not possible to pinpoint the scene of the accident from the surface vantage point. In this role, the aircraft are specially equipped to spot the scene and rescue or call for appropriate aircraft to rescue the injured persons.

Aviation is also important in the defence of nations and territories and in security surveillance to maintain peace. In these roles, various specialised aircraft are utilised to suit the roles that they play.

As can be seen from the above examples, aviation is steadily continuing to be entrenched into the activities of modern life. It is unimaginable that modern life would be as it is without the role played by the aviation industry.

Aircraft manufacturers and manufacturers of other equipment used in the support roles such as in air traffic control, weather forecasting, aircraft maintenance, and aviation training are continually designing and improving on the various products to make aviation safer and more efficient.

New types of aircraft in different roles such as in the carriage of passengers and cargo are on the drawing boards of manufacturers. Other features include higher speeds, low running costs (with improved fuel efficiency), and cost-effective maintenance.

The aviation industry is continuing to play a meaningful role in global trade. The transportation of people to visit potential trading partners and the transportation of goods and services are critical facets of air transportation. It is increasingly apparent that aviation is an important part of how the world does business now and in the foreseeable future.

Therefore, it is apparent that all sectors of the world economy do actually depend on aviation services at one point or the other. This is a demonstration of how important the aviation industry is to the world.

The foregoing chapters have explained the various sectors that make up the aviation industry and how the sectors are interconnected. It is notable that teamwork in the aviation industry is critical to ensure safety.

The importance of safety in the aviation industry cannot be overemphasised. In fact, the core of a well-managed aviation organisation centres on its safety procedures.

The achievement of safety standards and goals or targets depends largely on the plan and the training of personnel as well as putting them into practice. The achievement of a good safety record can add to good reputation. For those in commercial operation, it can mean increased business as your customers become aware that they are safe in your hands. This means that you put safety considerations first.

The way to achieve a complete safety concept begins with the training of personnel to ensure compliance with the safety program.

It is therefore reasonable to argue that training and a good safety record can yield rewards. Sometimes, it appears trivial or even monotonous when aviation safety is repeatedly emphasised. But when you consider the consequences of ignoring safety, you realise it is well worth enjoying adherence to safety procedures. An organisation would do well to instil in its personnel to enjoy safety practices.

There are so many reports of preventable incidents and accidents in the aviation industry In fact, they are too many to enumerate here. In some airline aircraft accidents, there were no survivors. Despite all the horrors and gruesome scenes of aircraft incidents and accidents, at least through incident/accident reports, we have had the opportunity to prevent them from happening again.

Safety must be a proactive event. If a crash is needed to get swift action on safety, then the flying public is getting far less protection than it deserves. It is worth noting that the safety regulations also protect the general public on the ground by ensuring that aircraft do not fall from the sky.

Overall, operators of aircraft, whether private or commercial, have their priorities. These can range from achieving a successful commercial operation to arriving or departing on time. Whatever priorities are adopted by whatever operator, aviation safety must be exercised to its fullest. Compromising safety procedures can sometimes lead to loss of compensation by insurance companies in the event of an incident or accident. In any case, greed for financial gain is a lousy excuse for an accident.

This book has covered the basic information for understanding what aviation is all about in general terms. For each sector of the aviation industry sectors, there are more details regarding the requirements of becoming a professional in a particular sector. If you just wanted to know a little about aviation, it is hoped that this book has achieved that. If you are looking for a career in aviation, however, then it is hoped that this book has aroused that interest in you. Seek further information on how to become an aviation professional in one of the disciplines described in this book. And if you are a beginner in your training stage, then it is hoped this book has given you some basic information about some sectors apart from yours. Aviation professionals are a breed unto themselves, and the indulgency in some is sometimes overwhelming. The famous Leonardo da Vinci quote may apply here: "When once you have tasted flight, you will forever walk the earth with your eyes turned skyward, for there you have been, and there you will always long to return."

Aviation professions are well worth pursuing as a career.

Bibliography

The World Fact Book www.wikipedia.org ICAO Annexes to the convention www.icao.int www.iata.org www.skybrary.aero

Travel News: www.travel-news.co.uk

ICAO Safety Report IATA Safe Skies Report Bombardier

Airbus: www.airbus.com
Boeing: www.boeing.com

About the Author

Fred Mabonga joined the aviation industry in 1975. Since then, he has had extensive training and experience within the industry and has worked for various airlines and a regulatory authority.

Trained in the United Kingdom at Brunel College and Oxford Air Training School, he obtained his aircraft maintenance engineer's licence in 1982 from the UK Civil Aviation Authority. He also completed the UKCAA airworthiness course in 1996. He obtained the UKCAA flight telephony operator's licence. He completed the IATA course on aircraft maintenance and engineering management in 1995 and the IATA course on human factors in aviation maintenance in 2003.

Fred has been an aircraft maintenance engineer for many aviation companies in various countries, and he has also held management positions including engineering manager and quality assurance manager at Air Namibia and Air Botswana. In 1983 to 1987, he was a technical instructor at Air Zimbabwe where he taught aircraft engineers. In 1998 to 2000, he was deputy chief of aviation safety at the directorate of civil aviation in Namibia. He was in charge of airworthiness and was chairman of the technical committee on aviation regulations. He has type training and experience on various aircraft from ATR42, Dash 8, BAe146 up to Boeing 747-400. He also has had training and experience on helicopters, including the Bell 427 and Bell 430 types. Fred has exposure to air-accident investigation and aviation safety training, working to prevent aircraft incidents and accidents.

He has experience in aviation technical consultancy and project management. He has a passion for aviation and is interested in training and promoting safety in the industry.

Printed in the United States
By Bookmasters